Review Tales
A Book Magazine For Indie Authors

Founder & Editor in Chief: S. Jeyran Main
Publisher: Review Tales Publishing & Editing Services
Print & Distribution: Ingram Spark
Designs: Pexels
ISBN 978-1-988680-66-8 (Paperback)
ISBN 978-1-988680-67-5 (Digital)
www.jeyranmain.com
For all inquiries, please contact us directly.

Contributors

K.T. Anglehart
JM Landels
Zachary Hagen
L. Ron Hubbard
Michael Hingson and Keri Wyatt Kent
Charles V Breakfield and Roxanne E Burkey
Jonni Jordyn
Tricia Copeland
Neil Perry Gordon
Robin Reardon
Ryan Schuette
Dr. Charles Michael Austin Ed.D.
Albert Seligman
John Tarrow
Rod Martinez
Precious Monèt
Sharon Curcio
Lakeea Kelly
Anthony Lo Cascio
Jennifer Lieberman

Photo Credits from Pexels:
bestasya-7909034
mahdi-chaghari-9996334-17300663
mentalhealthamerica-5530614

A BOOK MAGAZINE FOR INDIE AUTHORS

REVIEW TALES

Editor's Note

Spring is in the air, and so is the magic of storytelling! As nature awakens with bursts of color and fresh possibilities, so does the literary world bloom with new voices, compelling narratives, and timeless wisdom waiting to be discovered.

Welcome to the fifth edition of Review Tales, a celebration of books, authors, and the endless joy of reading. With thousands of books published each year, we carefully handpick the finest stories and bring you insightful reviews highlighting the best in literature. Whether you are searching for your next favorite read or seeking inspiration for your writing journey, this magazine guides encourages and uplifts you.

For writers, Spring is more than just a season; it's a reminder of renewal and growth. Each word you pen is a seed planted, and each story is a garden cultivated with care. Whether you're an aspiring novelist, a seasoned author, or an avid reader, remember this: great books don't just appear—they are written, rewritten, and polished with patience and passion. So keep writing, keep reading, and never underestimate the power of your words.

We hope this edition sparks new ideas, fuels your creativity, and, most importantly, reminds you why books remain one of life's greatest treasures. Here's to another season of literary discovery!

Happy reading,

Jeyran Main

Editor-in-Chief
Review Tales Magazine

SPRING 2025 | ISSUE 05

BOOK REVIEWS

Review Tales is thrilled to have reached the milestone of over 1,900 book reviews. With this extensive experience, we've had the privilege of exploring a vast range of literature. Our reviews are always impartial and thoughtfully crafted to highlight authors' strengths while inspiring them to keep creating. For this Spring issue, we've handpicked 20 exceptional book reviews to feature.

TO APPLY FOR A BOOK REVIEW VISIT
WWW.JEYRANMAIN.COM

Book Reviews

THE TWIN FLAME BY K.T. ANGLEHART

ALLAIGNA'S SONG: OVERTURE BY JM LANDELS

ETERNITY'S MIRROR BY ZACHARY HAGEN

WRITERS OF THE FUTURE VOLUME 41 BY L. RON HUBBARD

LIVE LIKE A GUIDE DOG BY MICHAEL HINGSON AND KERI WYATT KENT

THE KILLER ENIGMA BY CHARLES V BREAKFIELD AND ROXANNE E BURKEY

THE MOTHER OF ALL VIRUSES BY JONNI JORDYN

TO BE A FATE GUARDIAN BY TRICIA COPELAND

CHRONOSYNC: SCIENCE OF THE SOUL BY NEIL PERRY GORDON

FOR LOVE, BOOK 3 OF THE BLESSED BY ROBIN REARDON

AN END TO KINGS BY RYAN SCHUETTE

HOW TO FIND WORK FOR THE REST OF YOUR LIFE BY DR. CHARLES MICHAEL AUSTIN ED.D.

THE AMERICAN WEEKLY COVERS OF EDMUND DULAC BY ALBERT SELIGMAN

THE TALLISTON CHRONICLES BY JOHN TARROW

GRANDMA LUTHER KING BY ROD MARTINEZ

WITHOUT PASSION WHATS THE PURPOSE? BY PRECIOUS MONÈT

ASAYI AN AUTISTIC TEEN'S JOURNEY TO TOPPLE A SHOGUN IN MEDIEVAL JAPAN BY SHARON CURCIO

TRANSHERMATION BY LAKEEA KELLY

FOOD AS A PRESCRIPTION BY ANTHONY LO CASCIO

YEAR OF THE WHAT BY JENNIFER LIEBERMAN

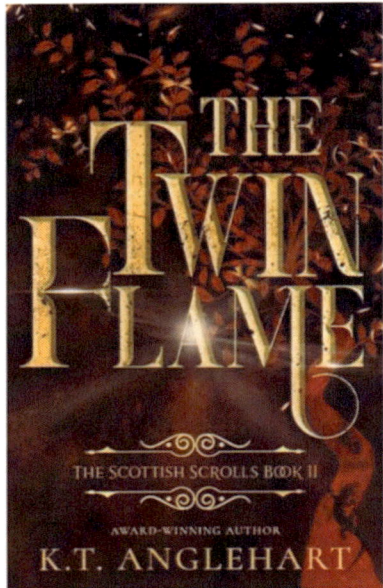

THE TWIN FLAME (THE SCOTTISH SCROLLS BOOK 2)

K.T. Anglehart

Reviewer: Jeyran Main

K.T. Anglehart's The Twin Flame is an enthralling continuation of the Scottish Scrolls series, weaving magic, adventure, and mythology into a story that grips the reader from beginning to end. Book 2 of this captivating series takes us deeper into Mckenna O'Dwyer's journey as she navigates her destiny as a witch. This time, the stakes are higher as she seeks answers about her past lives, her magic, and the prophecy that binds her to a dark fate.

Mckenna is a compelling protagonist—impulsive, fearless, and determined to use her powers to protect those she loves. As the story unfolds, Mckenna's magical education intensifies under the guidance of her mother, Abby, a powerful witch who reunites with her daughter after a long separation. Together, they begin to understand the full extent of Mckenna's abilities and the dangerous path she must follow. But Mckenna, driven by the need for more power, considers taking shortcuts to hasten her growth, supported by Cillian, a mysterious and persuasive ally.

The tension in the story builds as Mckenna grapples with the possibility of a catastrophic future where her powers might be used to destroy countless lives. Eachna, the white horse, brings visions of this devastating future, and Mckenna must decide whether the prophecy must be fulfilled or if there's another way to alter her destiny. The moral dilemma she faces—choosing between the lesser evil or risking everything for a chance at redemption—adds depth and intrigue to the plot.

The magic in The Twin Flame is rich and vivid, and the elemental powers Mckenna learns to harness are as complex as they are fascinating. The world-building continues to shine, and readers are immersed in the landscapes of Scotland and Ireland, where ancient folklore and powerful forces collide. The twists and turns keep you guessing, and the emotional depth of Mckenna's character ensures that her journey is one you will not forget.

With its passion, adventure, and supernatural elements, The Twin Flame is a must-read for fans of YA urban fantasy. Anglehart's storytelling continues to captivate, and the series is one of the most unique and engaging in the genre. If you loved the first book, you'll be hooked from the very first page of this thrilling continuation.

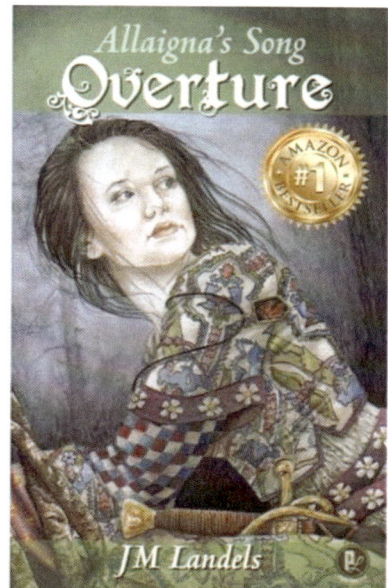

ALLAIGNA'S SONG: OVERTURE
JM Landels

Reviewer: Jeyran Main

Allaigna's Song: Overture by JM Landels is an enchanting start to a fantasy series filled with magic, mystery, and political intrigue. The story follows Allaigna, a young woman with a remarkable—and dangerous—gift: the ability to sing magic into existence. This powerful talent, inherited from her grandmother, is a well-kept secret, and Allaigna must navigate the complexities of her world while keeping her abilities hidden. The novel opens with a dark moment from her childhood when Allaigna almost sings her baby brother to sleep permanently, a chilling reminder of the strength and potential danger in her magic.

As she grows older, Allaigna takes on the role of a royal page, but the pressures of her secret and the weight of her family's mysteries make it challenging to live an everyday life. Her family has always been steeped in secrets, but as Allaigna begins to uncover more truths about her heritage, she realizes the stakes are much higher than she could have imagined. The tale is set against the backdrop of the Ilmar nations, where unstable peace and power struggles threaten the fragile balance of the land.

The narrative in Overture explores Allaigna's coming-of-age journey, during which she not only learns more about her magical abilities but also confronts the realities of her family's legacy. As Allaigna uncovers her grandmother's fate and the dangerous history of her magical lineage, she must choose whether to follow in her grandmother's footsteps or forge her own path, one that could either save or shatter the Ilmar nations.

Landels' world-building is rich and immersive, focusing on magic that feels integral to the story rather than simply a tool for spectacle. The characters, especially Allaigna, are well-crafted and relatable, making her struggles and growth deeply engaging for readers. The blend of magic, family drama, and political intrigue sets the stage for a captivating series that promises personal and grand-scale conflicts.

Allaigna's Song: Overture is a promising start to a series with potential for further adventure. Fans of magical realism and intricate fantasy worlds will find much to love.

ETERNITY'S MIRROR (ETERNAL CHRONICLES BOOK 2)
Zachary Hagen

Reviewer: Jeyran Main

Eternity's Mirror continues the thrilling saga of The Eternal Chronicles series, picking up right where Eternity's Well left off, and it does not disappoint. The story follows Elior, Nyx, and Opal as they confront new challenges while trying to uncover the mysteries of their world and beyond. With a growing obsession surrounding the enigmatic figure, Michael, the trio must navigate shifting landscapes and dangerous unknowns to resolve their dilemmas.

The Circle, an alliance that unites the countries of Lux Terra, is grappling with internal struggles, and as tensions rise, the group is tasked with finding Eliam—an essential figure in their journey. With time running out, they are forced to seek help from an unlikely ally, a disgraced magician, whose knowledge might be the key to unlocking the next phase of their quest. But when their plan goes awry, they find themselves on the other side of the Mirror of Eternity, entering a world filled with breathtaking wonders and terrifying dangers.

Hagen's world-building shines in Eternity's Mirror as readers are transported to a parallel realm unlike anything they could have imagined. The sense of awe and peril is tangible as the characters explore this strange and unpredictable landscape. The stakes have never been higher, and the team must rely on their courage and intellect to survive the cunning forces that seek to consume them.

The dynamic between Elior, Nyx, and Opal is further developed in this installment, with each character facing inner struggles and growth. As they confront external threats, their internal battles are equally important, making their journey all the more compelling. The introduction of the disgraced magi-technician adds a layer of complexity, and the shifting alliances and unexpected twists keep readers on edge.

Eternity's Mirror is a fast-paced, engaging continuation of The Eternal Chronicles, blending magic, intrigue, and high-stakes with rich character development. Fans of the series will be delighted by the further unraveling of mysteries, while newcomers will find plenty to enjoy in this exciting tale of adventure, magic, and survival.

WRITERS OF THE FUTURE VOLUME 41

L. Ron Hubbard

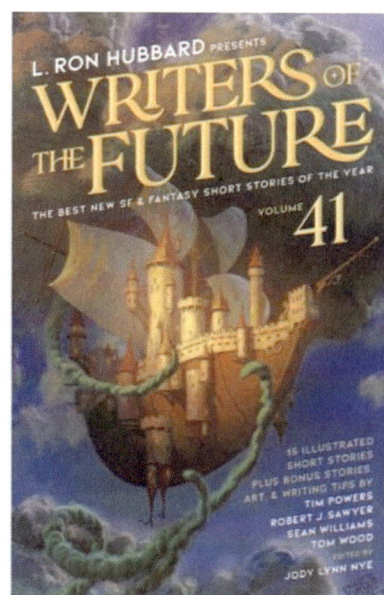

Reviewer: Jeyran Main

L. Ron Hubbard Presents Writers of the Future Volume 41 is an anthology that delivers on its promise to transport readers into the extraordinary. Celebrating the best new voices in speculative fiction, this volume offers an exhilarating mix of science fiction, fantasy, and thought-provoking narratives that push the boundaries of imagination. Whether you are a long-time series fan or a newcomer, this collection invites you to dive into a world of unexplored possibilities.

The anthology features gripping stories that span alien landscapes, futuristic technologies, and hidden realms. Each tale offers something unique, from time-traveling escapades to survival in dystopian societies. The protagonists are equally diverse, ranging from a young constable navigating a harsh alien frontier to a reclusive writer embarking on an unforgettable ride with a sentient car. These characters face seemingly insurmountable odds, and through their journeys, they redefine courage, resilience, and the human spirit.

What truly elevates this anthology is the stunning visual component. Every story is complemented by breathtaking original illustrations explicitly commissioned for this volume. These illustrations add depth and vibrancy to the stories and create a visual experience that immerses the reader in each narrative's world. The synergy between the words and images makes Volume 41 not just a literary collection but a visual and artistic masterpiece.

Additionally, the anthology offers valuable insights from established legends in speculative fiction, including L. Ron Hubbard, Robert J. Sawyer, and Tom Wood. Their essays provide a rare glimpse into the art of storytelling and offer inspiration to aspiring writers and creatives. These reflections on creative mastery add a layer of depth to the collection, making it an excellent resource for anyone interested in the craft of writing.

Volume 41 continues the legacy of the Writers of the Future competition, which has launched countless bestselling authors into the spotlight. This volume showcases rising talents shaping speculative fiction's future, offering readers a chance to discover tomorrow's stars today.

Writers of the Future Volume 41 is a must-read for fans of heart-pounding action, speculative storytelling, and beautiful illustrations. It's an anthology that will linger long after you turn the final page.

LIVE LIKE A GUIDE DOG
Michael Hingson & Keri Wyatt Kent

Reviewer: Jeyran Main

Live Like a Guide Dog: True Stories from a Blind Man and His Dogs about Being Brave, Overcoming Adversity, and Moving Forward in Faith by Michael Hingson and Keri Wyatt Kent is an inspiring and heartwarming book that offers profound life lessons drawn from the experiences of a blind man and his guide dogs. Michael Hingson, whose story captivated the world after he and his guide dog, Roselle, safely navigated their escape from the Twin Towers on 9/11 (a tale shared in his bestselling book Thunder Dog), now shares a deeper look into the lessons he's learned throughout his life with guide dogs.

In this new book, Hingson presents powerful insights into how we can live bravely and confidently, drawing from the unique perspective of working with guide dogs trained to overcome challenges and navigate obstacles. The central theme revolves around the surprising truth that fear, far from being something to avoid, can be a source of strength and preparation. Hingson encourages readers to embrace fear as a tool for building resilience, much like the guide dogs trained to face daunting situations with unwavering courage and determination. He illustrates how fear has become an essential tool in both his own life and the lives of his guide dogs.

Through moving stories, Hingson shares valuable lessons on how to equip ourselves to face life's trials. Whether we learn how to confront our fears, train ourselves to be brave, or find faith amid adversity, the book teaches us how to approach life with the same boldness and adaptability that a guide dog displays in its work. Hingson's reflections on overcoming obstacles reveal the universal struggle and thriving experience.

In addition to its inspiring content, Live Like a Guide Dog offers practical advice on developing personal courage, overcoming challenges, and maintaining momentum in difficult circumstances. Hingson's faith shines through as he shares how his guide dogs, especially Roselle, have helped him live a life of purpose and gratitude. His ability to find peace and strength in seemingly impossible situations is a testament to the power of living with faith, courage, and resilience.

A must-read for anyone seeking encouragement, Hingson's book proves that we can overcome even the most challenging obstacles with courage, faith, and a little guidance. It's a testament to the power of perseverance and the wisdom that can be found in embracing life's challenges.

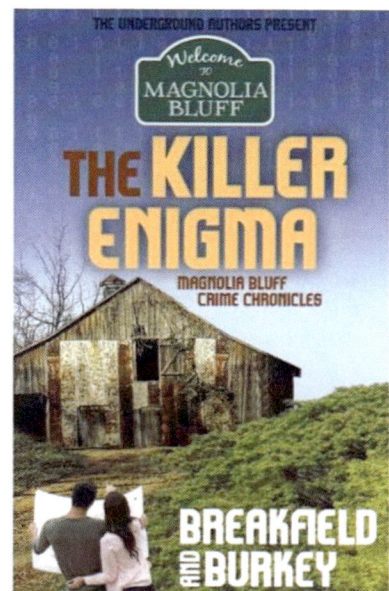

THE KILLER ENIGMA
Charles V. Breakfield and Roxanne E. Burkey

Reviewer: Jeyran Main

The Killer Enigma by Charles V. Breakfield and Roxanne E. Burkey is an exciting, fast-paced thriller that blends mystery, high-tech espionage, and the complexities of human emotion. The novel follows its protagonists' intricate investigations and technological battles, intertwining their personal lives with the high-stakes world of cyber threats and criminal intrigue. Breakfield and Burkey are known for their ability to weave complex storylines that captivate readers, and this book is no exception.

The story is set in a world where the dangers of cybercrime are more prominent than ever, and the characters must navigate a labyrinth of digital manipulation, hacking, and political intrigue. What makes The Killer Enigma stand out is how the authors build tension through their vivid depiction of high-tech gadgets, cyber warfare, and the deep, human element that drives the action. It's not just the technological threats that challenge the characters; it's also the emotional complexities of relationships and moral dilemmas they must face.

The protagonists are compelling and multidimensional. They grapple with their demons while trying to save the world from an ever-looming disaster. Their intelligence, resourcefulness, and emotional depth make them highly relatable, even in extreme danger. The dynamic between the characters—trust, betrayal, or collaboration—adds an intriguing layer to the plot, ensuring that readers are invested in the mystery and the character's fate.

At its core, The Killer Enigma raises questions about the role of technology in modern society and the ethical lines between right and wrong. It highlights the vulnerabilities of individuals, organizations, and even nations when faced with digital warfare. The authors excel at creating an atmosphere where nothing is as it seems and every move counts. The twists and turns keep readers on their seats, eager to uncover the truth behind the killer enigma.

Overall, The Killer Enigma is an engrossing thriller that explores the intersection of technology and human nature. It's an engaging read for fans of suspenseful mysteries, action-packed thrillers, and anyone interested in the darker side of technology. The authors' combined expertise and storytelling craft make this a standout in the genre, ensuring it will appeal to a wide range of readers.

THE MOTHER OF ALL VIRUSES: BOOK 1

Jonni Jordyn

Reviewer: Jeyran Main

The Mother of All Viruses by Jonni Jordyn delivers a heart-pounding, action-packed story blending cybercrime, conspiracy, and espionage. From the first chapter, readers are thrust into a world of danger, high stakes, and government intrigue. The story begins with an ex-hacker who becomes entangled in a series of events that spiral out of control after the theft of top-secret hardware. What follows is a complex, fast-paced narrative involving cover-ups, kidnappings, and the involvement of the FBI, CIA, and NSA.

The plot quickly escalates when the nation's defense systems are hacked, and the threat of Armageddon becomes more and more accurate. Jordyn expertly weaves these elements into an intricate web of suspense, forcing readers to keep turning pages as they try to make sense of the unfolding events. The involvement of a brilliant college professor adds another layer to the story, creating both intellectual and emotional tension that keeps the narrative engaging. This isn't just a story about hacking and government agencies; it's a tale of how far people will go when their lives—and the world—are at stake.

One of the most substantial aspects of The Mother of All Viruses is its unpredictability. When you think you have a handle on where the story is going, it throws another twist, leaving you questioning what will happen next. The complex characters, each with their secrets and motivations, further deepen the intrigue and drama, keeping you on the edge of your seat. Jordyn's ability to build suspense while layering in technology, conspiracy, and personal stakes is one of the book's most captivating qualities.

The book is perfect for fans of tech thrillers and government conspiracy stories. Its combination of espionage, high-tech crime, and emotional intensity creates a rollercoaster ride that never lets up. The plot's fast pace and the sense of imminent danger make it a thrilling read from start to finish. If you enjoy stories that keep you guessing, The Mother of All Viruses will deliver, making it a must-read for lovers of this genre.

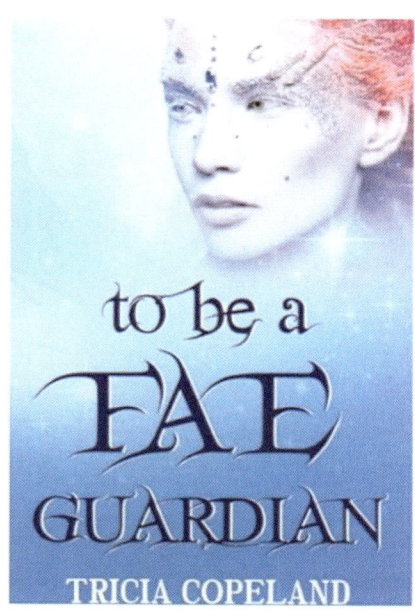

TO BE A FAE GUARDIAN
Tricia Copeland

Reviewer: Jeyran Main

To Be a Fae Guardian by Tricia Copeland is an enthralling tale set in a world where the Fae live alongside humans, hiding their true identities and powers. This novel is the second book in the Realm Chronicles series, following the journey of Titania, a mighty and determined young Fae warrior. The book blends elements of fantasy, action, and a touch of romance, making it an ideal read for Sarah J. Maas and Jenna Wolfhart fans.

At the story's core is Titania, a fierce and headstrong protagonist who has repeatedly proven that she will go to great lengths to protect her realm. In the first few chapters, we are thrown into an action-packed scene where Titania defeats a dangerous group of creatures threatening Middle Earth. However, in doing so, she violates two major edicts of the High Council, setting the stage for the following tension. The stakes are high, and Titania is under intense scrutiny as she grapples with her growing powers and the complexities of her responsibilities.

One of the book's most compelling aspects is Titania's internal struggle. While she is tasked with defending the realm, she is also burdened by a sense of duty and the consequences of her actions. The High Council, the governing body of the Fae, sees her as a potential liability, and they question whether she should be allowed to continue her role as a protector. Titania must navigate the intricate political landscape of the Fae world while also learning to master the powers that seem to grow stronger within her with each passing day.

The novel's pacing is brisk, with a balance of action scenes and moments of introspection. Copeland does an excellent job of building the world around Titania, using descriptive language to bring the Fae realm to life. The politics of the Fae world are as dangerous as the creatures lurking beneath the surface, and the author weaves these elements into the plot seamlessly.

The romance in To Be a Fae Guardian adds another layer of complexity to Titania's character. Her growing relationship with another Fae brings a sense of vulnerability to the otherwise tough and resilient protagonist. It also reminds us that even the most powerful beings have emotional struggles, adding depth to the narrative.

Overall, To Be a Fae Guardian is an exciting and captivating read that will keep fans of fantasy and adventure hooked. With its compelling characters, intricate world-building, and gripping plot, Tricia Copeland has once again created a world that readers will be eager to return to. Whether you are a longtime fan of fantasy or new to the genre, this book offers a thrilling ride that will leave you wanting more. It's a must-read for those who enjoy stories with complex characters, magical realms, and the ever-present battle between good and evil.

CHRONOSYNC: SCIENCE OF THE SOUL
Neil Perry Gordon

Reviewer: Jeyran Main

ChronoSync: Science of the Soul by Neil Perry Gordon is a captivating metaphysical thriller that combines science and spirituality. At the heart of the story is Dr. Adrienne Wallace, a brilliant scientist who invents ChronoSync, a revolutionary technology capable of unlocking the secrets of the soul's journey after death. This breakthrough device decodes hidden patterns within human DNA, providing irrefutable proof of past lives and forever altering humanity's understanding of existence.

As ChronoSync's discoveries spread across the globe, the world finds itself in turmoil. The implications of this revelation stretch far beyond the scientific community, sparking intense ethical debates, theological crises, and political power plays. Society is left grappling with profound moral questions, including the notions of karma, accountability, and whether individuals are responsible for the actions of their past lives. These questions challenge the very fabric of human identity and moral responsibility, pushing people to confront the mysteries of their existence in a way they never have before.

The novel doesn't just focus on the technological breakthrough but explores its profound impact on individuals and society. Dr. Wallace's invention forces humanity to confront the uncomfortable realities of its past and the possibility of reincarnation. The questions posed are not merely speculative but deeply personal, asking readers to reflect on their own lives and the actions that shape them. The political and societal consequences of ChronoSync's truth are far-reaching, sparking unrest as leaders and power players attempt to manipulate the newfound knowledge for their agendas.

What makes ChronoSync truly compelling is its invitation to readers to explore the deepest mysteries of existence. It is not just a thrilling story but a philosophical exploration of life, death, and the soul. The book asks readers to question everything they thought they knew about the afterlife, karma, and the power of human action. With its thought-provoking premise, ChronoSync: Science of the Soul challenges conventional wisdom while offering a gripping, intellectual narrative that will captivate fans of metaphysical thrillers.

Perfect for anyone intrigued by the convergence of science, spirituality, and the unexplored realms of human consciousness, ChronoSync will leave readers questioning the nature of their existence and the forces that shape their lives. It's a profound journey into what might lie beyond, daring to explore the very meaning of life and death.

FOR LOVE (BLESSED BE BOOK 3
Robin Reardon

Reviewer: Jeyran Main

In For Love, the third book in Robin Reardon's Blessed Be series, readers are taken on a poignant journey of self-discovery, love, and community. Spencer Hill, a compassionate Unitarian Universalist minister in the quiet town of Assisi, Vermont, has forged meaningful connections with his parishioners and a nearby Pagan community known as The Forest. Despite the warmth and friendship surrounding him, Spencer grapples with a deep, lingering emptiness in his heart.

Spencer has spent much of his life dedicated to others—his congregation, his loyal dog Klondike, and even a transgender teen named Kira, whose struggle for acceptance Spencer aids. While his life is entirely purposeful, his emotional fulfillment remains elusive. Spencer has never been able to forget his past love, a person who is now with someone else. His heart longs for a love that seems forever out of reach.

As Spencer pours himself into organizing a Pagan-inspired festival, he is drawn back into the complexities of his emotions. As she navigates her path toward self-acceptance, his connection with Kira provides him and the reader with moments of reflection on identity, love, and transformation. Yet, Spencer cannot avoid the painful reality of his unrequited love. Is he destined to remain alone? And how much is he willing to sacrifice for the chance at the love he's always wanted?

Reardon masterfully weaves themes of acceptance, love, and self-realization into this beautifully written tale. The characters' journeys unfold with depth and tenderness, leaving the reader rooting for Spencer and his quest for happiness. Spencer's story is one of hope and healing, demonstrating that love is not always straightforward but worth fighting for.

For Love can be read as a standalone novel. Still, for those who have followed Spencer's journey through the previous books in the Blessed Be series, this final installment offers a satisfying, emotional resolution to his character's arc. Reardon's writing resonates deeply with readers as it explores the complexities of human emotions, relationships, and the ongoing search for meaning and belonging.

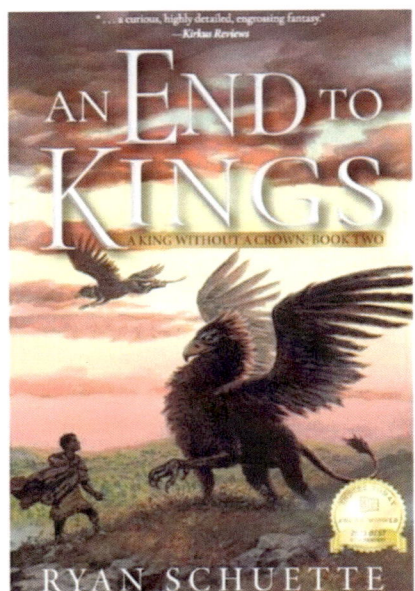

AN END TO KINGS
Ryan Schuette

Reviewer: Jeyran Main

In An End to Kings, the highly anticipated sequel to A Seat for the Rabble, Ryan Schuette masterfully concludes his gripping fantasy series, immersing readers again in the complex, war-torn kingdom of Loran. Set in the richly detailed world of Odma, where social injustice, wealth inequality, and ancient magic plague the land, this novel delivers a thrilling tale of political intrigue, family betrayal, and the quest for power.

At the heart of this narrative is Jason Warchild, a bastard prince determined to claim his birthright and transform the kingdom's oppressive structures. With his army of Cloudlanders behind him, Jason marches to the Kingstrials, a series of brutal trials in which he must defeat his rivals, including his fanatical uncle, Shaddon, to secure the throne. The trials are not only a test of martial skill but a fight for the very soul of the kingdom. Jason's journey has immense physical and emotional stakes, where failure could cost him the crown and his life.

The novel explores themes of class division and revolution, with Jason's rise to power symbolizing a larger struggle for the rights of the oppressed. His quest to dismantle the existing power structures is contrasted with the political maneuvering in the capital, where Princess Lorana Eddenhold navigates the dangerous game of court politics. As Lorana works to protect her half-brother from assassins and scheming nobles, she dreads the return of Prieslenne Edenia, a figure whose influence could tip the balance of power.

In the west, Rathos Robswell is tasked with uniting the fragmented factions of the Loyal Company, a mission that will either solidify Jason's cause or doom it to failure. Rathos' journey highlights the internal struggles of Jason's allies as they grapple with their motivations and beliefs.

Supernatural elements are also central to the story, with the mysterious sorcerer Zuran racing against time to confront the real evil threatening the kingdom. The stakes are high, and Schuette doesn't shy away from exploring the moral complexities of power, loyalty, and sacrifice.

An End to Kings is a thrilling conclusion combining political drama and fantasy. It offers readers a satisfying and thought-provoking end to a captivating series.

HOW TO FIND WORK FOR THE REST OF YOUR LIFE

Dr. Charles Michael Austin Ed.D.

Reviewer: Jeyran Main

In How to Find Work for the Rest of Your Life, Dr. Charles Michael Austin presents an essential guide for navigating the modern job market. Written with the changing dynamics of the 21st-century gig economy in mind, this book challenges outdated ideas about career security and loyalty to a single employer. In a world where corporate loyalty is no longer a given, the author offers practical advice on how individuals can take control of their careers and turn their skill sets into valuable, sellable brands.

Austin's book is a paradigm shift, encouraging readers to consider their business. Rather than relying on traditional career paths or corporate structures, Austin advocates for a new mindset in which people define and market their unique skills. The book highlights the importance of branding, self-awareness, and adaptability in an economy where job security is increasingly fleeting. It's a fresh take on career development, emphasizing self-empowerment and entrepreneurial thinking.

The book's core message is clear: you are the product and must learn how to sell yourself. Austin guides readers through identifying their strengths, crafting a compelling brand, and finding target markets willing to pay for their services. This approach can be applied to various professions and career paths, making the book valuable for anyone seeking work in today's unpredictable job market.

How to Find Work for the Rest of Your Life also stands out for its accessibility. The book doesn't overwhelm readers with technical jargon or overly complex strategies. Instead, Austin's writing is straightforward and practical, offering actionable tips that can be immediately implemented. Whether you're just starting your career, transitioning to a new field, or looking to enhance your existing work, this book provides valuable insights into building a lasting, flexible career.

Dr. Austin's book is a must-read for anyone who wants to thrive in the modern workforce. It's not just about finding a job—it's about creating a sustainable, fulfilling career that lasts for as long as you want. If you're ready to take control of your future, How to Find Work for the Rest of Your Life is the perfect guide to get started.

THE AMERICAN WEEKLY COVERS OF EDMUND DULAC 1924–1951: 100TH

ALBERT SELIGMAN

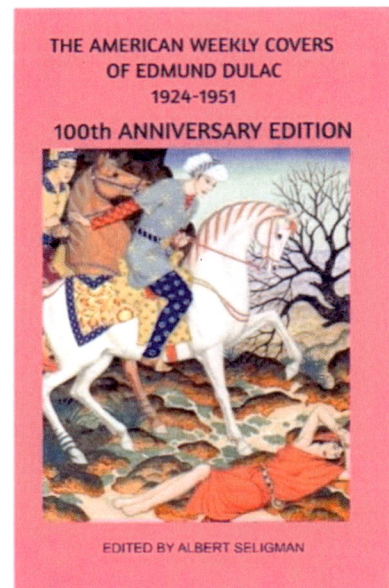

Reviewer: Jeyran Main

The American Weekly Covers of Edmund Dulac 1924-1951: 100th Anniversary Edition is a breathtaking tribute to one of the most influential illustrators of the Golden Age. Albert Seligman presents a compelling collection of Dulac's work, focusing on his lesser-known but equally stunning magazine covers. While Dulac is widely celebrated for his watercolor book illustrations, this edition highlights his contributions to The American Weekly, a popular Sunday magazine that showcased his artistry to a broader audience.

This collection serves as a historical record and a stunning visual experience, preserving Dulac's incredible talent in a new light. His mastery of color, composition, and storytelling through imagery is beautifully displayed in these magazine covers, each one capturing the imagination and elegance that defined his career. Unlike many of his contemporaries, Dulac adapted to evolving printing technologies, utilizing the advancements in color separation to create depth and vibrancy in his works. This allowed his watercolors to translate more effectively into printed media, making these covers unique art pieces.

Seligman's meticulous attention to detail in curating and presenting this collection makes this book a must-have for collectors, historians, and fans of classic illustration. He provides a well-researched introduction that explores Dulac's journey from France to England, his transition from book illustration to magazine covers, and the historical context of early 20th-century illustration. Readers gain a deeper appreciation for Dulac's ability to adapt and innovate within an ever-changing publishing industry.

One of the most remarkable aspects of this edition is its high-quality print replica format, which allows readers to appreciate the richness of Dulac's color work. The book not only preserves his legacy but also highlights the importance of magazine illustrations when print media was at its peak. The covers are beautifully reproduced, ensuring that Dulac's intricate details and dreamy atmospheres remain as captivating as they were when first published.

Whether you are a longtime admirer of Edmund Dulac or just discovering his work, The American Weekly Covers of Edmund Dulac 1924-1951 is an exquisite collection that deserves a place on any art lover's shelf. This book is more than just a showcase of stunning illustrations—it is a testament to the lasting influence of an artist whose work continues to inspire generations.

THE TALLISTON CHRONICLES

John Tarrow

Reviewer: Jeyran Main

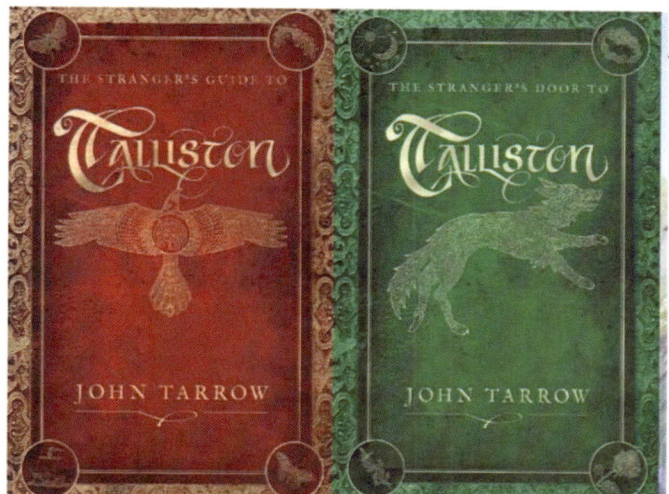

THE TALLISTON CHRONICLES by John Tarrow are captivating YA adventures that blend mystery, magic, and rich historical settings into an unforgettable experience. These books transport readers to a world filled with labyrinths, secret doors, and various magical realms, all intricately woven with exciting adventures and complex characters.

The Stranger's Guide to Talliston opens with thirteen-year-old Joe, who finds himself trapped within a mysterious council house that becomes a labyrinth leading to magical realms. Each door in the maze unlocks a different world—from Victorian Britain to 1950s New Orleans—creating a diverse and expansive backdrop. The heart of this story lies in Joe's journey, not only through these varied realms but also in his search for his missing parents. As Joe battles sinister forces and uncovers the secrets within the labyrinth, readers are drawn into an emotional and magical adventure that explores themes of loss, family, and personal growth. The book's grounding in the extraordinary Talliston House and Gardens, dubbed "Britain's Most Extraordinary Home," adds a rich, atmospheric layer to the narrative, making the setting feel as alive as the characters.

In The Stranger's Door to Talliston, Tarrow expands on the universe he created in the first book, revisiting several realms while introducing new settings and characters. The narrative shifts to 1590, where we follow thirteen-year-old Bríane as she attempts to save her grandmother from execution for witchcraft. Set against the backdrop of Elizabethan Essex, Bríane's quest to find a magical grimoire at the crossroads of all worlds—the Forest of Doors—adds a new layer of intrigue to the Talliston universe. With more rooms and secrets to uncover, this second installment deepens the labyrinth's mysteries. It introduces thrilling new characters and adventures that keep readers hooked until the last page.

Both books are a brilliant mix of historical fiction, magic, and adventure. Tarrow's world-building is exceptional, with rich landscapes and deeply immersive storytelling. The character development, particularly of Joe and Bríane, offers readers relatable, influential figures to root for. Whether you're a fan of YA, fantasy, or historical fiction, these books will captivate your imagination and take you on a thrilling, magical journey.

GRANDMA LUTHER KING
Rod Martinez

Reviewer: Jeyran Main

Grandma Luther King by Rod Martinez is a beautifully illustrated and heartwarming children's book that brings history to life in an engaging and accessible way. Through the lens of a young boy's journey with his African American grandmother, the story unfolds an essential chapter of the Civil Rights Movement, showcasing the impact of activism and the power of memory.

The story begins with a young boy on a city bus with his grandmother, who passes a building that sparks curiosity. What unfolds is a heartfelt conversation about the building's significance. During a civil rights protest years ago, Black students organized a crucial sit-in to challenge restaurant segregation. The twist? His grandmother was one of those brave students who participated in the protest.

Through her eyes, the young boy learns the power of activism, sacrifice, and standing up for what is right, even when faced with adversity. The story offers a compelling reflection on the civil rights struggle, framed through the relatable relationship between grandmother and grandson. Martinez does an excellent job of presenting historical events digestibly for younger audiences, ensuring they grasp the importance of equality and activism while maintaining a gentle, nurturing tone.

Catherine Purcell's charming illustrations reinforce the book's powerful message. The artwork complements the narrative beautifully, capturing the emotion and significance of the story with vibrant, expressive visuals. The writing and illustrations work harmoniously to create a memorable reading experience for children and adults.

Grandma Luther King is not just about history—it's about family, legacy, and the courage to make a difference. It teaches young readers the value of activism and the strength of their voices. The book serves as a reminder that each generation has a role in advancing justice and equality.

This book is a perfect resource for teaching children about the Civil Rights Movement and the importance of standing up for racial equality. It is an inspiring and empowering tale that will resonate with readers of all ages, encouraging them to reflect on their own in shaping the future. Martinez's storytelling and evocative illustrations make Grandma Luther King an exceptional read that will leave a lasting impression on young minds.

WITHOUT PASSION, WHAT'S THE PURPOSE
Precious Monèt

Reviewer: Jeyran Main

Without Passion, What's the Purpose: 5 Keys to Fuel the Fire That Burns Within You by Precious Monèt is an inspiring guide for anyone feeling lost or disconnected from their Purpose in life. In this powerful and motivational book, the author reflects on her journey of self-discovery, offering wisdom and practical advice for those looking to reignite their passion and find meaning in their lives.

Monèt draws from her personal experiences and insights to highlight the importance of purpose and passion, arguing that they are deeply interconnected. She explains that living your purpose without passion is impossible for those struggling with a sense of emptiness or stagnation; this book serves as a wake-up call to reconnect with what truly drives them.

The book is structured around five essential keys designed to help readers uncover their strengths, tap into their intuition, and ultimately discover their true life's purpose. These keys offer actionable steps to unlock happiness, embrace your innate potential, and maximize the impact of your passion. One of the most potent aspects of Monèt's message is that she emphasizes the importance of using passion for personal fulfillment and achieving success and profit. She encourages readers to align their love with their goals to achieve satisfaction and prosperity.

What sets Without Passion, What's the Purpose apart is the practical yet deeply introspective approach that Monèt takes. The book doesn't just offer abstract theories or motivational phrases but gives readers concrete tools to begin their journey toward personal transformation. Through exercises and reflections, readers are guided to dive deep within themselves to uncover what truly excites and motivates them, leading them to live a life aligned with their Purpose.

Monèt's writing is authentic and relatable, making it easy for readers to connect with her journey and the lessons she imparts. Whether you feel unfulfilled in your career, relationships, or personal life, this book reminds you that the path to a fulfilling life starts with passion. It is a call to action for those ready to stop living on autopilot and begin pursuing their true calling with vigor and enthusiasm.

In Without Passion, What's the Purpose, Monèt offers hope and guidance for anyone seeking to transform their life, ignite their passion, and step into their purpose confidently and clearly. If you're ready to fuel the fire within you, this book is an excellent resource for starting that journey.

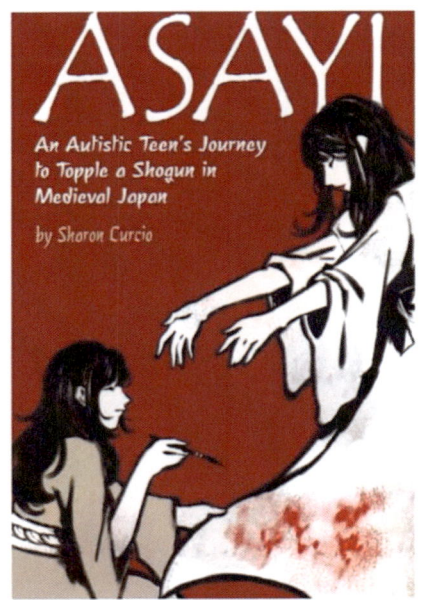

ASAYI
Sharon Curcio

Reviewer: Jeyran Main

Asayi: An Autistic Teen's Journey to Topple a Shogun in Medieval Japan by Sharon Curcio is a compelling and emotionally charged historical novel that offers a fresh perspective on medieval Japan, seen through the eyes of an autistic young woman named Asayi. The story delves into the harrowing challenges Asayi faces during harsh political unrest and social inequality. Asayi, vulnerable yet resilient, is the unexpected hero in a world that often marginalizes different people.

Set against a backdrop of court intrigues and political turmoil, the novel explores the struggles of the underdogs—those from various walks of life who are often overlooked by society. Asayi is thrust into a deadly game of deception, where loyalty is tested, and survival is a daily battle. The interplay between political agendas and personal survival is intense, making the reader feel the full weight of the stakes involved.

What makes the novel unique is its portrayal of an autistic protagonist in a time when understanding and acceptance were scarce. Asayi's experiences of vulnerability, isolation, and the search for belonging are depicted with great sensitivity, making her character feel authentic and relatable. Her resilience and ability to form meaningful connections are central to the narrative, showing how someone who might have once been considered an outsider can become an agent of change.

The novel also incorporates elements of traditional Japanese culture, such as the ghostly figures that appear throughout the story. These figures symbolize the enduring presence of the past and the ghosts of societal wrongs. These supernatural aspects are seamlessly woven into the story, adding depth and intrigue.

Overall, Asayi is a remarkable tale of survival, courage, and resistance. With its rich historical setting, vivid characters, and a protagonist who faces both personal and political battles, the novel will captivate readers who appreciate stories of resilience in the face of adversity. It is a journey of self-discovery, loyalty, and triumph against injustice—truly a must-read for fans of historical fiction and those looking for a fresh, diverse perspective in the genre.

TRANSHERMATION: HOW GOD CAN TAKE EVERYTHING YOU'VE BEEN THROUGH AND TRANSFORM YOU FOR HIS GLORY!

Lakeea Kelly

Reviewer: Jeyran Main

TransHERmation by Minister Lakeea Kelly is a powerful and profoundly moving account of overcoming depression and experiencing spiritual transformation through the grace of God. Kelly's journey from darkness to light, brokenness to wholeness, offers readers both hope and practical steps for healing, making this book a valuable resource for anyone struggling with emotional pain, shame, or a sense of unworthiness.

The author's story begins in her late twenties when she faced a mental health crisis that plunged her into a deep depression. This depression was fueled by guilt and shame over past sins, causing Kelly to question the worthiness of God's forgiveness. She felt tormented by painful memories, flashbacks, and the belief that God was punishing her. Her openness in sharing these vulnerable moments makes her story relatable and shows that even the darkest times can lead to profound transformation.

What stands out in TransHERmation is Kelly's insight into how depression begins with a single negative thought, often planted by the enemy, which grows and distorts one's perception of themselves and their relationship with God. This resonates deeply as readers learn that it is not the situation itself but how we interpret it that determines our emotional state. Kelly describes how God's light, like the rising sun in Psalm 4:18, broke through her darkness, leading her to fight for her life through the power of the Holy Spirit.

Kelly's transformation is physical and spiritual as she shares her journey of deliverance and healing. TransHERmation is a testament to God's faithfulness in completing the work He began in her life, and it showcases the power of perseverance, faith, and prayer. Kelly's story of moving from captivity to freedom, from spiritual blindness to emotional wholeness, is inspiring and offers valuable lessons for those seeking a similar healing journey.

This book is filled with practical steps for connecting with one's true identity and purpose in Christ, offering tools for deliverance from rejection, ungodly soul ties, and emotional scars. It's incredibly empowering for teenage mothers, their parents, and anyone who has faced emotional or spiritual hardship. With powerful prayers, wisdom, and relevant lessons throughout, TransHERmation is more than just a memoir—it's a guide to finding healing and purpose through God's transformative power.

This book is a beacon of light for anyone seeking hope, strength, and spiritual healing. It shows that true transformation is possible through God's grace.

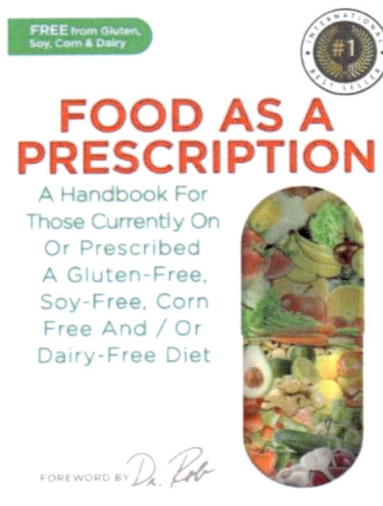

FREE from Gluten, Soy, Corn & Dairy

FOOD AS A PRESCRIPTION

A Handbook For Those Currently On Or Prescribed A Gluten-Free, Soy-Free, Corn Free And / Or Dairy-Free Diet

FOREWORD BY *Dr. Rob*

ANTHONY & STACI LO CASCIO

FOOD AS A PRESCRIPTION
Anthony Lo Cascio

Reviewer: Jeyran Main

Anthony and Staci Lo Cascio's Food As a Prescription is more than just a dietary guide—it is a deeply personal and empowering resource for those navigating food-related health challenges. Unlike many nutrition books that focus solely on what to avoid, this book takes a holistic and hopeful approach. It provides practical solutions and personal stories that make the advice relatable and achievable.

As professional dancers, the Lo Cascios faced chronic health issues that affected their careers and overall well-being. Through years of trial and discovery, they realized food wasn't just fuel or comfort but a key to healing. Their struggles with food intolerances led them to uncover life-changing dietary adjustments, and their willingness to share these experiences makes this book unique. Readers aren't just given a list of restrictions; they're offered a new perspective on food as medicine and a tool for reclaiming health.

One of the book's strongest points is its accessibility. The Lo Cascios present their insights in an easy-to-understand, step-by-step manner. Transitioning to a gluten-free, soy-free, corn-free, or dairy-free diet can be overwhelming, but the book helps break it down into manageable steps. It covers meal planning, grocery shopping, and handling social situations while maintaining dietary needs. There are also tested recipes, making adapting to a new diet achievable.

Another standout feature is the discussion on mindset. Many dietary books focus on elimination and restriction, but Food As a Prescription encourages a shift in perspective. Instead of seeing diet changes as sacrifices, the book emphasizes empowerment and self-care. Readers are reminded that they are not alone in their journey and that intentional, consistent changes can lead to profound health improvements.

At just 88 pages, the book is concise yet packed with valuable information. It's ideal for those newly navigating food intolerances and those refining their dietary habits. With a blend of personal stories, practical tips, and encouragement, Food As a Prescription is not just a book—it's a transformational guide to better health. Highly recommended!

YEAR OF THE WHAT?
Jennifer Lieberman

Reviewer: Jeyran Main

Year of the What? by Jennifer Lieberman is a bold, humorous, and heartfelt romantic comedy that captures the journey of self-discovery and the complexity of relationships. The novel follows Dana, a 25-year-old woman struggling to move on after a breakup that left her heartbroken and uncertain. Six months later, Dana is navigating life as a single woman in New York City, searching for the one but unsure of what she truly wants or needs. A self-described "virgin once removed," Dana feels trapped by societal expectations, trying to suppress her desire to be the "good girl."

Enter Kelly, Dana's uninhibited and unapologetic roommate, who embodies confidence and freedom. Kelly is a brilliant woman who drops out of college to pursue a life that is anything but conventional—becoming a dominatrix in a Chelsea dungeon and making "lawyer money." Her adventurous spirit and carefree attitude profoundly impact Dana, pushing her out of her comfort zone and encouraging her to explore her desires and curiosity.

As Dana embarks on an unexpected journey of sexual exploration and personal growth, she begins to confront her insecurities and embrace her true self. Throughout the novel, Lieberman skillfully blends humor, romance, and a bit of taboo to tell an entertaining and thought-provoking story. Dana's evolution is the book's heart as she navigates the complexities of intimacy, personal identity, and empowerment.

Year of the What? It is not just about sexual discovery but also about learning to accept and love oneself. Dana's adventure reminds us that true happiness and fulfillment come not from external validation but from embracing who we are. Lieberman's writing is witty and relatable, with a cast of vibrant characters that make the book delightful and engaging. The mix of humor, romance, and exploration is perfect for anyone looking for a story that pushes boundaries while remaining grounded in the universal quest for self-empowerment.

A global award winner, including the 2022 Global Book Awards Gold Medal for Coming of Age Books, Year of the What? Will leave readers reflecting on their journey of self-discovery long after they turn the last page.